FEATHERSTONE
Bloomsbury Publishing Plc
50 Bedford Square, London, WC1B 3DP, UK

BLOOMSBURY, FEATHERSTONE and the Feather logo are trademarks of Bloomsbury Publishing Plc

First published in Great Britain 2019 by Bloomsbury Publishing Plc
Text copyright © Penny Tassoni, 2019
Illustrations copyright © Mel Four, 2019

Penny Tassoni and Mel Four have asserted their rights under the Copyright, Designs and Patents Act,
1988, to be identified as Author and Illustrator of this work

A catalogue record for this book is available from the British Library

ISBN: HB: 978-1-4729-6670-4; ePDF: 978-1-4729-6671-1; ePub: 978-1-4729-7434-1

2 4 6 8 10 9 7 5 3 1

Printed and bound in China by Leo Paper Products, Heshan, Guangdong

To find out more about our authors and books visit www.bloomsbury.com and sign up for our newsletters

Time to Make Friends

Penny Tassoni
Illustrated by Mel Four

FEATHERSTONE
LONDON OXFORD NEW YORK NEW DELHI SYDNEY

It's good to have friends.

Every friend is different.

Friends play together.

Who do you play with?

Friends can have adventures too.

What adventures can you see?

There are other things that friends like to do.

Cook together.

Eat together.

Laugh
together.

Sing and
dance together.

Friends also...

Sit side by side for story time.

Learn new things together.

What do you do with your friends?

It's good to have a friend when you're feeling sad.

Before.

Has a friend helped you?

After.

You may also need a friend when you...

Fall over.

Feel sick.

Need help.

Want to
go home.

Sometimes friends don't want to play.

Some may even move away.

Then it's time to make new friends.

Watch and see how they play.

They may play a different way.

Don't push in!

And remember you
can't always win.

Being kind is important too.

Can you see how being kind helps you to make friends?

Always look out for
other children who
may need a friend
like YOU!

Notes for parents and carers

Making friends is important for young children. Most children's early friendships are based on play interests but by three years old, many children will have preferred friends. As children develop, friendships become very important. For children to make and stay friends, they need a range of skills that you can help them with.

Helping your child to make friends

- Make sure that your child gets to play with a variety of materials and toys regardless of gender. This means that they will have more play interests and so more potential playmates.

- Play games with your child that require turn taking. Waiting for a turn is an essential skill.

- Don't always let your child win or have their own way. Children need to learn to lose and also give and take.

- Organise times when your child can play with children of a similar age.

- Encourage your child to share some of their toys and also to ask other children what they want to do.

- Role model positive comments so that your child learns to say positive things to other children, e.g. 'I like the way you can bounce the ball.'

- Help your child learn about the motives and feelings of others. Share books and ask questions about why someone may be feeling sad or happy.

- Use everyday opportunities to talk about feelings.

- Don't worry if your child doesn't have a best friend. Young children's friendships can be quite fluid.